"God Is

"God is not pleased with what's going on in some Pulpits." And He has a special punishment for those "Preachers" who lead His children astray.

Freddie Lee Caldwell

Text copyright © 2013 Freddie Lee Caldwell
Cover Illustration copyright
© 2013 Howard McClary

ISBN-13: 978-1482331523

This book is dedicated to those who practice the art of being a preacher, and ministering a church.

People to acknowledge: all those who put up with my weird way of thinking, and allowed me to be around them so I could learn.

My Life Mentors:

Denver Charles Caldwell (My Father)

Catherine Caldwell (My Mother)

James Mamba McCuller (My Friend & Mentor)

Daddy Melvin McCray (My Friend & Mentor)

James H. Norman (My Boss, Friend, & Best Man)

"God Is Not Pleased!"

Freddie Lee Caldwell

Table of Contents

Introduction

Chapter One   I am for the "Preacher"

Chapter Two   Holy Ground

Chapter Three   People vs. Position

Chapter Four   A God of Solution

Chapter Five   What you must do now?

Chapter Six   Preach On Sister

Introduction

As a young man, living, and growing up in Central Florida, I was exposed to the church, church activities, and church personnel, especially the Preacher.

My mother was always going to church (3-4 times per week). My father was very active in the community and in the church. I knew the many churches in my community, and my father knew all the preachers.

People have always said some preachers were all about the money! Even in the old days when people did not have money the preacher was going to people's houses to eat. This has been said all my life, and in many cases it has been true.

The members of the church have always taken good care of their preacher.

In the 21st century church there has been an increase in men (and women) entering into the "Fulltime Ministry Industry".

The reason is the amount of money that is hoarded by the industry professionals:

fulltime preachers. So much money is exchanging hands in the churches across America today it makes one wonder: "How would Christ react?

Mark 11: 15-17:

15) *And they come to Jerusalem: and Jesus went into the temple, and began to cast out them that sold, and bought in the temple, and overthrew the tables of the money changers, and the seats of them that sold doves;* 16) *and would not suffer that any man should carry any vessel through the temple.* 17) *And he taught, saying unto them, Is it not written, My house shall be called of all nations the house of prayer? But ye have made it a den of thieves.*

It is interesting how Jesus Christ had more trouble with the Pharisees/ Preachers of His day than He had with the actual devil! So why are we so tolerant of the same kind of characters today?

I have also known some great preachers who, from my observations, were honest and up-right men. As I became an adult, became active in the community, and got to know many of the preachers in the Rochester, NY community, I have seen both sides of this coin.

Over these years of exposure to this world, and through some of my own life experiences, I have come to the conclusion that I had to prepare this letter for the preacher.

I do believe that God wants me to write this letter to the preacher. Since I am not a preacher I can write this letter from a more non-conventional perspective.

I like to look at things from the perspective of people in the streets now sitting in the pews of the church. That man or woman who has never experienced life in the church setting, and are now ready to make this big change!

I know that as a public speaker no preacher in his right mind is going to allow anyone to share this information in a church setting. No Way!

What I mean is this kind of information rocks the boat, and nobody wants to rock the boat!

This would cause real problems in a newly developing church.

People might say I don't like preachers. Throughout this book I plan to remind you that I have the utmost respect for preachers. This book is dedicated to Preachers everywhere.

So, I am sharing this information in book form. For those who want it, they can get it through reading for themselves. Just remember the information in this book is for the preacher!

I have never sat in the Pulpit so I can't say how this will go over up there. But all my life I have sat in the audience of the church. I have heard some of the things I will talk about, and I have seen some of the things I will talk about.

Doing the research on this book I was amazed at the information available on this subject. It appears that many people across America and around the world have similar concerns.

The WWW has all one would need…but it is spread all over the place under many different topics and key search words.

My attempt was to bring together much of the information into a useable form, for the purpose of this book, and its readers.

I know that God is not pleased with what is going on in some of the pulpits. I am also sure that God is not pleased with how the preachers of the gospel are living, when you compare the living standards of the shepherd (the preacher), to that of the sheep (church members).

Prayerfully find out what you are by the things you do, (even in your private life) and from the messages you preach.

Whether or not you do the same things that Jesus Christ has done, and preach the same kind of messages that Jesus Christ preached?

If the answer is yes then you are placed by God in His church. Continue to do the faithful work.

If your life and your sermons contradict that of Jesus Christ then it is time for you to repent. You don't want to be another Judas Iscariot.

Heb. 10:31 *"It is a fearful thing to fall into the hands of the living God."*

This book is to help the preacher of the 21st century look at himself/herself, and look at the flock he/she is charged with caring for; to decide if he/she is going to continue on the road he/she is on, or does he/she plan to change course; to see if there is a more impactful way he/she can shepherd the flock.

This book is also to assist that preacher who wants to change after completing the assessment of himself/herself, and his/her church.

This book can assist the new preacher who is just starting in the ministry, and wants to do it right the first time.

I have been complaining about this issue for a long time and have done nothing. God was getting me ready for what is to come from some of my preacher friends. I have many!

Prayerfully God has prepared the preachers who will be impacted by this book, and their hearts will not be hardened against me.

This book will cover four things:

1. God is not pleased with the activities preachers allow in the pulpits across America.
2. God is not pleased with the way preachers are living in comparison to the members.
3. God is not pleased with the way the preacher is spending his money in support of God's work here on earth.
4. God wants to see it change "NOW", and here is where you start "Preacher".

The last chapter in the book takes a look at women in the pulpit. My research will explore the pros and cons of this issue.

Why has this issue caused so much confusion for so long?

The whole issue comes to your interpretation of the Bible.

If what you believe, combined with what you read, support your belief that women should preach then go for it.

Whenever this discussion would come up, and people would start to share their opinion, one of my preacher friends would say, "Brothers, you better leave them girls alone!"

Disclaimer to Everything:

The information I share is not mine, I read it somewhere, heard someone say it somewhere, and some of it I may have thought of myself. But even that belongs to God so it belongs to all of you. So if you say something I said belongs to you, you are correct, and you will hear nothing from me.

FLC

Chapter One

"I am for the Preacher"

Many years ago there was a program called *"Star Trek"*, with Capt. Kirk, Dr. Mc Coy, Zulu Spock, and all those proud members of the "Starship Enterprise".

There was one episode where the team landed on the surface of this strange planet.

Deep in the planet this entity determined the moment you set foot on the planet; what you liked most, and what your deepest desires were.

Then this entity would send these robots to the surface; they would tell you what you most desired, and promise you they could deliver; if you would only allow them to touch you.

These robots looked just like what you loved and talked like just the one you always wanted. All you had to do was allow them to touch you, and call your name.

The moment the robot touched the one they were designed for, that person would fall dead. The robot would say, "I am for Kirk", Zulu would fight that one. The robot that said, "I am for Spock", and Kirk would fight with that one.

They had to all make sure they were never touched by the robot that was designed for them. With this effort the team had time to plan an escape.

I am for the preacher. I am the robot that says, "I am for the Preachers of America." God has sent me to speak with the preacher. I have to do this for the preacher!

I do this for the preacher because all my life I have been close to them, loved, and respected them.

My father was what you call a "Jack Leg" preacher. He knew the Bible, so he went all over central Florida preaching.

My big brother is a preacher, and both of his sons, are preachers. All my adult life I have had jobs that involved working with preachers. Many of my friends are preachers.

God did not design me to talk to the rich and famous about how they spend their money, to support God's work.

God did not design me to talk to the rich and successful sports figures.

God told me to talk to the preacher about how he is spending his money to support God's work.

God knows that it takes money to run the world!

God knows that men love money. That is why he requires us to give Him 10% off the top of ours.

God knows that it takes money to pay for the care of the old, the young, the sick; those who cannot, and those who will not take care of themselves.

All these are God's children, and their care is your responsibility preacher!

Although my touch is not deadly to the preacher it is supposed to make him think, and hopefully change his ways.

My father used to tell me, "Boy if you throw a rock over there in that hog-pin ain't but one pig gonna holla...that's the one you hit!"

So all my preacher friends don't get mad with me. If the shoe doesn't fit, don't wear it!

If the stones I throw don't hit you, don't holler!

The work of running the world must go on. We all know it's going to take money.

I have to tell the preachers how God is watching him and how he spends his money in support of God's work here on earth.

My preacher and friend told me to be aware of people coming up to you telling you that God told them to tell you something.

"You better sprinkle some salt on that before you eat it! God ain't sent all these people who say God sent them." (Rev. James Cherry)

God has told me to get this information to the preachers, but the sheep in the flock need to hear this too. Because many of them are thinking about becoming a preacher themselves, because it looks like preachers are living so well!

Becoming a preacher may not be what they really want!

Many Preachers are not aware of the special punishment God has planned for preachers who lead His children astray.

God is not pleased with some of the things that go on in the pulpits across America!

If this word gets to the preachers of America, it will go around the world. The preachers of America are in contact with preachers around the world.

They work together spreading the gospel around the world, and I know if America's preachers take this conversation seriously everyone will get the message.

So the Preachers of America are my target. "I am for the Preacher!"
I am not a preacher, but I love them, and the great job they are doing spreading the

Gospel. They are doing a great work. A work God has called many of them to do.

Many of them were not called by God; they were sent by their mothers!

Preaching the gospel is a noble profession, and many enter into it just to earn a living. Others have no choice but to do it.

God called many of them, and others just went!

The American preacher has made many connections around the world, and when the American preacher sees the error in their ways, the world will see it too.

My message pertains to how the preacher spends his money to support God's work here on earth.

I pray that all preachers tithe their incomes as they instruct their members to do.

This is not the money I am referring to preachers. I am referring to the money you spend in other places, doing other things, while many of your members are suffering.

Solomon was the king who built God's temple. While he was working on God's house he was also working on his own. God had to put Solomon in "check" when he was spending as much time, and money, on his own house as he was spending on God's house.

I am calling all you preachers who this may apply to into "check". Compare your home to some of the homes some of your members are living in.

I don't mean your members are supposed to live the life style that some of you live. But you and I both know God's children should not be living the way they are.
You can do something about it!

Some of you Preachers across America make some enormous incomes; and rightfully so.

What I am saying, my friend and preacher, is use your heart and make a simple comparison.

Too many Preachers are living too well on the blessings that God is sending through them. Those blessings are not supposed to stay with him and his family. They are supposed to flow through him, and his family, to feed God's children.

My father once told me, "People can do wrong for so long, until they think it is right"! They will fight you, or have you kicked out of the church, if you oppose them.

Plus, most of the preachers are concerned about what the people in their church hear, and who they hear it from.

They are the shepherd charged with the protection of all the sheep under his care. He had better protect them! He had better be concerned about what they hear!

There are many preachers who feel they are closer to God than any member of the church. This is not always the case.

There are some members of your church closer to God than you will ever be. Take advice from some of those members. They can assist you in being a better person. Not that you are a bad person, but you can become better.

There are many preachers who feel they know everything, and will never admit they are wrong. Many times you are wrong preacher! Admit it, and move on! You are a people too!

You can make a mistake, and you don't know everything.

For example, preachers you have to admit that you are the ones that for many years have taught the members of your congregations that sex was bad.

God created sex, and made it enjoyable for those who are married. It is one of the ways that a married couple strives to become one. It is used to develop a good working relationship between a man and wife.

Over the years you preachers have made sex a bad thing. This is the reason it took twenty years for the church, and its preachers, to begin telling its members about HIV/AIDS.

Think where we would be in the battle against this dreaded disease, if we could have gotten the church involved sooner!

American Greed

There is a thing called "American Greed." It has no treatment nor does it have a cure. Once you are infected by it you will take it to your grave, or it will take you to your grave.

All segments of American society are based on greed.

Washington D.C., where our laws are made, all decisions are influenced and guided by money, and the lust for more.

In New York City, down on Wall Street, through which all the money flows, actions are taken, and all decisions are influenced and guided by money, and the lust for more.

In your city and mine where we all work, play, and spend the little money we have all decisions are influenced and guided by money and the lust for more.

I know you would like to think your church and all the decisions on how long you are going to be in service on Sunday, will the preacher be available for consultation this week, can I call my preacher and have him pray for and/or with me today is influenced and guided by money, …and the lust for more.

So my message is for the preacher, "God is not pleased"!

He told me to tell you that you are blessed with the ability to preach the gospel. You are gifted with a way to help people understand the word of God. You are then rewarded with a number of sheep to shepherd.

Some of you have thousands of members. Some of you may only have one hundred, but they are all precious to God.

Your blessing brings money into the church, which is not your money to spend the way some of you preachers are spending it!

As the shepherd you are to make sure everything you have (including your money) is used to make sure the sheep in your charge do not go wanting for anything.

Lead them to still waters so they can drink; Make them to lie down in green pasture so they can be refreshed; Your rod and your staff are to comfort them (that includes your money)!

In the Bible days people did not always have money. Their wealth was determined by how many animals they had, or how much land they controlled or how many people they had working for them. Everyone lived off of the land.

Those who did not have were somehow provided for, and cared for.

Preacher, are you sure all your sheep are cared for? How many of your sheep are wanting for some real basic needs?

God is not pleased with some of the things that go on in the pulpits of America.

We have liars up there, we have homosexual persons up there, and we have whore mongers up there. We have out right thieves up there, and God is not pleased!

I hear preachers say sometimes, "Are there any preachers in the church, you can come up front!" Preacher you don't know what, or who you are inviting up there into holy ground.

My mentor "Daddy Melvin" used to say, "Son, the bottom of hell is going to be covered with preacher's skulls." He said "Hell is 1500 miles long, and 1500 miles wide. That's a lot of skulls!"

The preacher has all those tailor made suits and that real fancy car that cost $100,000.00. His wife brags about how many $500.00 bags and hats she owns.

They are living in a million dollar home.

They are living off some of the money the members should be getting back through the church providing assistance for some sheep in wanting.

Please preachers, nobody said you and your family should not live well. God wants all his children to live well.

Some of you are adding new parts to the church, to make it larger, and more beautiful than your fellow preacher's church across town.

You have not had a full church in years. I don't know why you need a larger building, and more seats?

That money could, and should be spent helping some of your members.

You have members in your church that don't have food in their home and Preacher you don't know their names! God is not pleased!

It is your responsibility to make sure all the members of your church are doing well. But instead you have to go to Texas to do a revival, for which you will be getting paid.

You have to go to do a speaking engagement in another city, for with you are getting paid.

You are part of a preacher's conference and somehow you are getting paid, or this is a free trip to just hang out with some other preachers.

Don't you care what they are hearing? Don't you care about what they are saying about you?

I am afraid that a lot of preachers across America have the greed disease. All they want is more money!

God can cure anything, including greed.

I am afraid that a lot of preachers do not know what the special punishment that preachers are going to get.

God looks at shepherds and preachers in a different way than the way He views sheep and church members.

The shepherd is charged by the owner of the sheep to protect them, even at the cost of his own life.

God has charged you preachers with the responsibility of protecting your members, even at the cost of your life, and your money.

God is not pleased with what is going on in some of the pulpits across America. And He has a special punishment for the preacher who leads His children astray.

You preachers are spending too much of your money on you, and your family, and not nearly enough on feeding the sheep.

Across America there are new members joining churches, and they will be gone back to the streets in two months. Why?

What is going on in the church that new members don't stay?

What is going on in the churches that young people leave the church at the age of twenty?
What is going on in the church that men will not attend?

Why is the church full of women only?

Why is it that half of all marriages in America are ending in divorce?
Does the church have anything to do with that?

They are getting married in the church!

These and other things that happen in the churches of America today are the reasons why God is not pleased.

It is the preacher who is the leader of the church and all members look up to him, or her. They need to know, and remember, what God has in store for them if they don't change, and fast!

That is why I am for the preacher, and I must get this message out.

Chapter Two

"Holy Ground"

In many religions the raised platform reached by steps, from which the speaker speaks is considered Holy Ground. This area in the church is sacred, and any and everybody can't go up there. This raised platform is also called the pulpit.

Such a platform is mentioned in connection with the gathering of the people of Israel to hear the reading of the Law of God, and its interpretation.

(Neh. 8:4.) In the King James Version of the Bible, *"Holy of Holies"* is always translated as *"Most Holy Place".* This is in keeping with the intention of the Hebrew idiom to express the utmost degree of holiness.

The King James Version of the Bible has been in existence for nearly five hundred years.

For most of that time it was a primary reference in much of the English speaking world for information about Judaism.

Thus, the name *"Most Holy Place"* is used to refer to the *"Holy of Holies"* in many English documents.

One has to be careful about who stands by you when you are in the pulpit. In *Neh. 8:4* there was a lot of other people standing on the right side and the left side of Ezra the preacher.

In *Exodus 3:5* Moses was commanded to remove his shoes for he was standing on Holy Ground. It is a place held sacred for special purposes.

The word "Holy" means *"exalted, or worthy of devotion."* A place that is perfect in Goodness, and Righteousness.

The pulpit is such a place, especially when the Bible is open.

The pulpit is a place that is divine, venerated, and sacred. A place used in combination with taking oaths.

For example, the airplane that the President travels on is called Air Force One. It does not become Air Force One until the President comes aboard.

Some do not consider the pulpit holy ground until the Bible is opened. Or that platform does not become holy until some good person occupies it, the preacher.

Look at the types of people preachers allow to stand in holy ground. God is not pleased.

In modern and ancient times many things have been called holy or sacred: Holy city, holy communion, the holy day, holy ghost, and holy spirit, etc.

In the Masonic Lodge there is a place considered holy ground where no one goes at anytime. Masons are trained to walk around this area.

In the temple built by Moses and the children of Israel, there is a place called the holy of holies, and the High Priest can enter it only once a year.

When the high priest enters this holy of holies he has a rope tied around his waist,

so if anything happens to him while he is in there they can pull him out.
Only certain people can go in there!

There must be strict attention paid to who stands, or enters holy ground.

God is not pleased with the things that happen on holy ground (the pulpit), and the children are being lead astray from this holy place.

This special punishment is awaiting these preachers who are using it as a playground.

Jeremiah 21:14 says, *"I will punish you according to the fruit of your doings, saith the Lord: and I will kindle a fire in the forest thereof, and it shall devour all things round about it."*

I am afraid that many preachers are using the holy ground for a playground. They stand in the pulpit, and beg for money to do strange things that doesn't please God, nor does it feed the sheep they are responsible for protecting, and providing for.

Pimping from the Pulpit

This can be one of two things : A pimp who uses exhortation and persuasion to keep his women doing his bidding , or a preacher who is NOT truly called, but uses a gift of gab to fleece his flock , and instead of helping his congregation, or the poor, is busy lining his own pockets.

Down in the neighborhood when we say pimp we are referring to those who earn their living talking others into working for them, or to keep money flowing in their direction.

It happens when drugs are sold, when clothes are stolen, and then sold to the people in the community.

There are those who say the preacher of a church is pimping the people. Driving luxury cars and dressing in designer suits, and not really working for it.

In most cases a pimp is a ruthless character that will do anything for a dollar. Anything! He also expects his followers to do anything for a dollar, or anything to please him. (Bully)!

The old song about crossing over one by one; God is bringing the pimps out of His pulpits across America, one by one.

You don't want to be one of those preachers who God catches with your work undone.

Every month we see on TV, or hear in the news, about another preacher God is putting his deeds out into the light.

God is bringing them down one by one.

In this town, like many others across America, pimping from the pulpit is a very good business.

If you listen you can hear the preachers talking about the money their church has, and how the "Building Fund" is maintained. How much of it is his.

You can hear them brag about the money they "earn", the cars they can buy (or have bought), the clothes they wear, and how much they cost.

They talk about how certain members scramble to be the preacher's pet.

They even brag about the women in the church who want them, or how they can have them any time they want.

They talk about the single women in the church who are heads of the different groups of workers that make up the church family. Ready and willing to do their bidding!

God is not pleased with the activities that take place in the pulpit. That is supposed to be "Holy Ground" up there!

God is not pleased about some of the things that happen as a result of what goes on in the pulpit.

It is one thing to have a preacher abusing the congregation with lies and trickery, and also having people sitting up there that are known homosexuals. God is not pleased!

All the big preachers of America now have their wives as ministers too, and getting a salary from the church…which is all part of the game.

Many of them have other friends and relatives getting into the business, which is all good I suppose.

Rev. Bob Harrington of New Orleans, LA says that" Homosexuals should be a part of the church, but not in the pulpit. We should pray for them, not make leaders out of them!"

My big brother is a preacher, and he always says I don't like preachers. This is not true of course. I just call it like I see it. I feel that preachers are an important part of the community, but many people do not trust them, and with good reason some of the time.

Anyone who loves the Lord, and spends some time watching how business is handled from the pulpit will tell you that something is wrong.

I have heard many preachers say that God will handle his business in due time. That no one can take care of God's business better than God Himself.

I came by to tell the preacher that it is time to take care of the business of your church, and feed the sheep of the church.

God is attempting to handle His business by assigning me to talk to the preachers while there is still time.

I feel I have been getting ready for writing this letter all my life. This is why I have always had a special love for the preacher. I hope that this message is received well, and acted upon.

When did Jesus become not enough?

The Sunday morning service is full of extras to keep people coming and paying because the pimp preacher does not believe that Jesus is enough.

The churches' services of today include the best singers and musicians in your town; you observe the spooky communion service, the fake laying on of hands, and the dancing mimes.

There is no one to blame because all the churches are doing it. Jesus is not enough anymore!

The Bible tells us to praise the Lord with music, singing, dancing, and praying; but this is a bit much when it is not real.

There are those who are moving from church to church looking for the one thing that is missing. The pimp in the pulpit from his throne on high can see the faces, and he knows when you are thinking about leaving. He does nothing because he knows that the spell has worn off.

He can see that you have stopped saying amen, clapping, shouting, jumping, fainting, convulsing, lusting, and running around the church on the command of the preacher, or you hear that music that says "Shout."

The pimp in the pulpit is under increasing pressure to keep the church service intriguing, and exciting.

The fear is that he may lose his members to that new light-skinned pretty preacher down the street, or across town.

That is why all the theatrics. Jesus is no longer enough!

It has come to the point where the supply and demand principle that dominates the business world also dominates the church world.

The pimp preacher will continue to give the pew what it wants in return for what the pimp preacher wants, "Money."

If you have not been kicked out of a church, or found some reason to leave one, you are agreeing with what the pimp preacher is doing.

What people want brother preacher is a real encounter with Jesus Christ, and to join hands with, and learn from fellow believers. I can assure you that they do not want the synthetic version.

Jesus Christ is enough for me!

One of the things that I dislike is when the money plate is passed, and people put in the plate what they have, or what amount they choose, and the preacher asks for more.

Beg for more, pimp more out of the people.

God loves a cheerful giver. But now the people are being asked for money they don't have, or not willing to give.

But the preacher embarrasses them into giving a little more, and this money given unwillingly does no good for the church, or the giver.

That money will not do the pimp any good either, but he feels that he has done his job.

I love God, and I love the church. I do truly love my preacher, because he is my friend too.

They all need to evaluate where they are, and what they are doing to a poor and unsuspecting people looking at them, listening to them, and obeying them.

God is not pleased! He told me to tell you He is not pleased, and He has a special punishment for you preacher. But, there is still time!

Where is the discipline?

Webster defines discipline as *"training that corrects, molds, or perfects the mental faculties, or moral character. A control gained by enforcing obedience, or order, an orderly, or prescribed conduct, a pattern of behavior."*

In today's society there is no discipline. Parents don't discipline their children anymore; the children decide what they are going to eat; they decide what activity the family is going to engage in, and what will be watched on TV.

These same children go to school and many of them receive good grades, but their behavior is disrespectful and disruptive in the classroom, and the teacher does nothing.

Where is the discipline?

On the job the parents of these children are suppose to work from 8am-5pm, but they arrive to work at 9 am, and go home at 3 pm. The supervisor does nothing, nor says anything to that staff person as the rest of the staff watch, and wait for some disciplinary action to be taken.

Very soon all the staff production is down because there is no discipline.

In the political arena nothing gets done for the people because our government leaders are stealing the money, engaging in sexual misconduct, and no one is disciplined.

These same leaders have children at home, and some of them belong to a church somewhere.
In the churches people are watching the preacher do everything that is not pleasing to God, and the membership will not, or in many cases, cannot discipline the preacher.

These same preachers have children at home, and the children are watching their parents.

So the members come to church like they want to, when they want to, and this attitude comes to Sunday school with the children.

Where is the discipline in the American society? God is not pleased!

The American society's building blocks begin in the home, spreads to the school, church, community, city, state, and nation.

Parents are supposed to control their homes, and they receive some of that training in the church, and on the job.

This book is not about the pattern of behavior on the job, or the moral character of the politicians, but it is about the pattern of behavior in the church.

As the definition of discipline states molding moral character should start with you preacher.

Your members cannot hear what you are saying because you are making so much noise doing what you are doing, and God is not pleased!

Chapter Three

"People vs. Position"

When Jesus was about to leave and go back to Heaven, He instructed the preachers whom He had trained to "Feed His sheep." To provide them with all they needed; protect, and comfort them; and I believe that meant money too!

After this group of people received the "Holy Ghost" they went out in all directions spreading the story of what they had witnessed.

All those that believed, and followed them, the preachers of that time had to provide them with what they needed.

In the Bible days people did not use as much money as we do today. Their need was more items, services they could use right now.

Today we need money to pay for those items, and the ability to go, and acquire them.

They are to be provided by the shepherd, for the sheep.

Just like the shepherd would give all he has to protect his sheep, the preacher must be prepared to give all he has, even his life, for his sheep.

In this book we are seeking to help the preacher understand that giving his money to help the members of his church is what is expected of him or her.

The preacher is gifted in speech, and teaching the people what the word of God means. If the preacher uses this gift well, he will be rewarded with all he needs.

By teaching the people the preacher brings money into the church. As a result of these good teachings the people bring their tithes into the warehouse, (the church) and there is enough for all to prosper.

The preacher is blessed with money in modern times, but that money is not all his to keep. Some of it is to be used to feed the sheep, and to provide them with what they need.

Take a good sermon of your favorite preacher. Take a sermon of Jesus Christ. You may take a portion of the Sermon on the Mount, or any one of His other teachings from the Bible.

Compare the sermons. If the purpose and concept of the sermons are geared in the same direction, then you have a good preacher. If there is discord then you have a false preacher.

Many preachers are paid a salary to oversee the church. That money is to provide for him, and his church family.

Being a preacher is different from having a job. On a job you work and bring home money to take care of your family.

The pay a preacher receives is for his church family. The job is for your family, a preacher's money is for the flock!

Although I am aware that many preachers think this is a job. That is the reason being a preacher is such a special occupation.

If you think preaching is a job you were not God called. That is the difference between the people, and the position.

Those who are called by God understand that money is for them to feed the sheep, and not live lavish lives.

That money is not to be spent building new churches, when you can't fill all the seats you have.

I am trying to get the preacher to understand the church is the people, not the building.

Spend the money helping the people in the church, and then the people will help you take care of the building.

Many times this is why the preacher and his family lived in the house next to the church. The preacher and his family lived in the house next to the church, and that house was part of the church's responsibility.

Being in the position of preacher has become more significant than the people, and God is not pleased.

God told me to tell you that if your members are taken care of, and they are not wanting for the basic things of life, preacher you will do very well!

When God said He wanted us to live life, and live it abundantly, He meant it just that way. Abundance is more than enough, not lavish greed.

Example: if you are a family of three, and three pieces of fish is enough, five pieces is abundance. If you have twenty pieces of fish, you are being greedy, and you should share with those in need.

The bite of John the Baptist's moral challenge is hard for us to appreciate today. His command to share clothing, and food (Luke 3:11) with those in need was a painful jab at a society that was hungry to acquire material objects.

He warned the tax collectors not to take more money than they had coming to them (Luke 3:12-13); he exposed the greed that had drawn persons to such positions in the first place.

He told the soldiers to be content with their wages, and not to use their powers to take advantage of the common people (Luke 3:14).

The preacher of today is more concerned about his position in the community.

Some things that determine his position is the size of his church, how many members he has, the position he holds in the preacher's conference, how well he can sing or pray in public, and what kind of speaker he is.

Jesus has told you about those public prayers, and what they get for you: nothing but the praise of man, and sometimes a good collection.

In 2013 the leaders of many flocks are more concerned about their position and their title than they are about feeding the sheep.
The preacher doesn't want to be called the preacher anymore. He now wants to be called Bishop or Apostle, etc.

Many don't want to be called Reverend anymore. It is the position and title, not the responsibility, or duty.

My research tells me that a preacher is one who delivers a sermon with much exhortation in an officious or tiresome manner; one who proclaims the gospel, the proclamation of God's saving work through Jesus Christ.

Many places in the bible the preacher and the bishop are defined as the same. In other places they are very different.

The bishop is called a clerical official who superintends other clergy. The bishop is called an overseer, an elder, or pastor charged with the responsibility of spiritual leadership in a local church.

In the Greek, bishop was used to refer to local gods that watched over the people, and or a country.

Noah was called a preacher of righteousness.

Solomon described himself as a preacher who taught words of truth.

Jonah and all the prophets of the Old Testament were regarded as preachers.

Jesus referred to Himself as a preacher.

Jesus also called his disciples preachers.

I think it is a cool term.

There are various kinds of preachers for God preaching many kinds of messages with love, compassion, excitement, emotion and charisma. They are very convincing. Is it possible that they could be false?

Read what Jesus Christ says: Matt 7:21: *"Not everyone that saith unto me, Lord, Lord, shall enter into the kingdom of heaven; but he that doeth the will of my Father which is in heaven."*

The true preacher for God is the one who does the will of the Father who is in heaven.

The will of the Father for Jesus Christ was to die on the cross.

The will of God for the preachers are to take their own cross, and follow Jesus Christ.

"Matt 26:42: *"He went away again the second time, and prayed, saying, O my Father, if this cup may not pass away from me, except I drink it, thy will be done."*

The will of the Father for a true preacher is to preach the Word of God truthfully, but not for personal gain.

The will of the Father in Christian ministry is to present the Church perfect, and complete in all the will of God. If a preacher does not keep himself pure, and does not gear his ministry to make the people perfect for the Lord, then that church is not given to him by the Father in heaven.

As glamorous as it is, that church was his own making. Most of the preachers across America are building fantastic, spectacular, masterpiece ministries in the name of God for themselves. Col 4:12: *"...always labouring fervently for you in prayers that ye may stand perfect and complete in all the will of God."*

The will of the Father in someone's personal life is to keep their sanctification, which is moral purity.

Why is it that the modern day preacher's position has become so important that he is no longer a preacher?

The distinction between preacher and teacher made in the church today is not evident in the New Testament. They are the same.

There are people in the churches today who drive to church on gas fumes, because they have no money to put gas in the car. They want to make sure they bring their tithes to the church.

Many of these people have no food in their homes to eat, but they trust in the Lord to provide as promised.

The preacher stands in the pulpit and teaches/preaches the word, and does not know anything about the people they are responsible for protecting.

The preacher does not know the names of his members.

They will talk about kicking a person out of the church because they cannot pay their church dues, and tithes.

The members are afraid to ask for a session with the preacher or a church leader because they have been unable to pay their dues.

These are the first things the church looks into before scheduling a session for a member.

God is not pleased! Hear me preachers, God is not pleased!

In some of these large churches a member has to make an appointment, and go through three other people before they can talk to the preacher.

The preacher will not accept an appointment if the member has not paid their tithes, or they are behind in their dues.

This member needs counseling, and advice, but most of all they need some money to pay the gas, and electric. They need some money to make a car note, or they will lose their transportation.

The preacher is too busy making money for himself to take care of the people. Or he is doing something to enhance his position.

The preacher of today is more concerned about the next book he is writing, or the tapes he wants you to buy; trying to get the members to get enough money to go on a cruise, and they can't pay their bills.

They love their preacher, and try to do whatever he asks of them.

This is what he has taught them to do. This is why he will receive that special punishment.

He is leading God's children astray.
Preacher you do not want to get on the wrong side of God!

I am trying to get the preacher to evaluate how he spends his money advancing God's work here on earth, before Jesus returns.

I want the preacher to look at his money, not the church's money. I want him/her to address their greed.

There is a special punishment awaiting the preacher who does not take care of the sheep assigned to him.

I am not sure you understand what the "FEAR" of GOD means. I am not sure that some of you Preachers are afraid of God.
I mean scared of Him!

Read your Bible and see some of the awesome things this God can do, and will do to you for leading His children astray.

I was sent to make you stop and think, there is still time to turn this thing around Preachers. Hear me! Please!

Are you a prophet for God, or a prophet for profit?

"I will punish you according to the fruit of your doing!"

The money you receive through the church is to feed the sheep. What is the food the sheep need?

The preacher of today does a good job praying for the people. The people need prayer!

The preacher does a good job teaching the word. The people need teaching!

Some of the members need one-on-one treatment from the preacher. Many preachers provide guidance for their members.

But if you really talk to them they will tell you what they need, and many times that is financial help.

The church should provide that, and if you stop thinking about the next trip you are taking, the next addition you want to make to the building, or the next way to make some money for yourself, you will see the real needs of your members.

Solomon Burke, the blues singer said, *"You have to be looking for a sign".* Preacher if you are not looking for a sign, you will never see the sign! You have to be looking!

The sign is that the people are getting fed up with the way things are going. There is rebellion in the air.

The young people leave the church as soon as they are from under the leadership of their parents.

The men have given up on coming to church, only the wives come. That is one of the reasons why the church of today is full of women.

Preacher, are you looking for the signs?

The church did not officially begin until the day of Pentecost. One of the things done on church days of old was to collect an offering for the needy.

All the belongings of the members were brought to the church, and every member's needs were attended to.

Does the church of today collect an offering for the needy, or does all the money go to the greedy?

The church is the building for public worship where the religious body's needs are attended to, and the members receive their religious rites.

There is rebellion in the air preacher; an opposing, or taking arms against a ruler or government.

The members of many churches are about ready to disobey, to oppose the ones in authority, and in control. They are ready to renounce, and resist by force. They feel anger, and revulsion.

We have all witnessed the change in governments around the world.

When I was in the world of work the company I was part of had a Head Start program. This is where we educated young children before they started school, providing them with a head start.

The rules mandated that we not only work with the children, we had to also educate the parents so they could provide support to their children when they entered first grade.

These were parents that never had power over anything.

We taught them that they had power. We taught them what that power was, and we taught them how to use that power.

The parents of the Head Start children learned that they could stop things from happening, and they could make things happen.

Who do you think they tested their newly found power on first: the ones who taught them about power?

In many cases this was a good thing, and in other cases it was a constant source of confusion.

This is the very reason preachers don't teach their members that they have power because they will test it on the preacher, and the leadership of the church.

Instead the preacher teaches the members that the preacher has absolute power. We all know what happens when someone has absolute power, they become corrupt absolutely.

Your members have a right to expect support from the church. Your members have a right to determine how the church's money is spent. As members come to understand this, our churches will change, and I believe for the better.

God is not pleased with what is going on in the pulpit.

Well, what is the answer to this problem? What is it that God wants you preachers to do to change what is going to happen soon?

We all know that God would not sight a problem without a solution right at hand.
We also know that change is very hard for anyone, especially for someone who has been doing it wrong for so long that they think it is right.

I do care if you do this, but remember what my preacher said about listening to people who say God told them to tell you something.

Remember also that greed is a disease, and you have it preacher, you have it. There is no cure, nor is there any treatment, and you will probably die with it, or from it.

God is a God of solution!

Chapter Four

"A God of Solution"

As I stated earlier, I am not a preacher, but I do love studying the Bible. For those of you, who do not believe God is a God of solution, let me site a few examples.

The Flood

Problem: God was not pleased with His creation of man, and how he (man) was conducting himself.

Geneses 6:5: *"And God saw that the wickedness of man was great in the earth, and that every imagination of the thoughts of his heart was only evil continually."*

Solution: God caused the flood to clean up the whole thing.

Geneses 6:7: *"And the Lord said, I will destroy man whom I have created from the face of the earth; both man, and beast, and the creeping thing, and the fowls of the air; for it repenteth me that I have made man."*

God is not pleased with the conduct of the preacher, and the things he/she allows to happen in the pulpit, or the message that emanates from this holy place.

Because the preacher is the leader in the church, the things they do and say are repeated by the members.

Many preachers tell the members not to do as they do, but to follow the laws of the Lord.

This is just what most members do, they do as their preacher does, because they trust them, and admire them.

Your members can't hear what you are saying preacher because you are making so much noise doing what you do!

This wickedness is spread throughout the church family. The love of money is an evil thing, and because of that love the preacher and the members do evil to one another.

Throughout this book we have observed some of the things that happen; things that God is not pleased with, and things that cause evil.

God has asked me to remind the preacher of this evil, and to warn him of the punishment to come. I believe it will be coming shortly, and there is still time to change.

The preacher must take this message for what it really means, and act accordingly.

This book is designed to point out some of the wrong things God is not pleased with, to suggest a method and process of change, and to remind the preacher of the special punishment in store for him/her.

The Tower of Babel

Problem: God was not pleased with the whole earth being of one language.

Genesis 11:6: *"And the Lord said, Behold, the people is one, and they have all one language; and this thing they begin to do: and now nothing will be restrained from them, which they have imagined to do."*

Solution: God fixed it where they could not speak to one another.

Genesis 11:7: *"Go to, let us go down, and there confound their language, that they may not understand one another's speech."*

The language used by preachers, and the methods are all the same everywhere. The love of money and fame is a goal of many preachers around the world.

The training that preachers receive to deceive the people are all the same. They teach each other how to avoid paying taxes on their enormous fortunes.

They teach each other that making their wives preachers too will bring even more money into their households.

They teach each other how to use this gift of "gab" to deceive the members of their churches into doing more for them, and getting more money into the church with which they line their pockets.

God is not pleased, because He gave them this gift to help the people, to lead them to Christ. But instead, they use this gift for the enrichment of themselves.

The people at the "Towel of Babel" had no fear of God, because they did not know him. Some of the preachers of today do not fear God. This fear must be re-established in the preacher, and in the people, because we do not want God to come, and confound the language again.

Or, God may do something else this time. (???)

We all know that the true word of God will be preached to the people. If you do not do it preacher, someone else will. God can make the rocks preach the word!

Many preachers have so much money and fame that they think they are above the law of man and God.

Remember we serve a God of solution, and He has an answer to this situation too!

Many preachers of today act as though they are gods themselves. They do not act on behalf of the people, but for themselves.

One indicator is when the preacher starts to say "MY CHURCH", instead of saying our church, or the church.

God is not pleased, and we do not want Him to come and get things straight. This is why I am for the preacher, and this message is for the preacher.

God is giving you an opportunity to make these changes now.

The Exodus from Egypt

Problem: God was not pleased with the treatment of His children in Egypt.
Exodus 3:7: *"And the Lord said, I have seen the affliction of my people which are in Egypt, and have heard their cry by reason of their taskmasters; for I know their sorrows."*

Solution: God brought His people out of bondage, and put them in a land of milk and honey.

Exodus 12: 36 & 37: *"And the Lord gave the people favor in the sight of the Egyptians, so that they lent unto them such things as they required. And they spoiled the Egyptians.*

And the children of Israel journeyed from Rameses to Succoth, about six hundred thousand on foot that were men, beside children."

As in the time of Moses, God is not pleased with the cries He is hearing from His children.

The members of your churches are crying for help, and guidance that only their preacher, and their church can provide.

God's children are being abused by their preacher. I know because I have heard the preachers brag about how they manipulate their members.

Many of you, like the burning bush, will burn, and not burn up. Many of you will receive lashes across your backs, and the lashing will not stop.

With every lash you will be reminded of this warning I am trying to share. This has to be God speaking through me, because it is surely not me talking.

Like Pharaoh, some of your hearts will harden when you read these words. Some of you will say that I am mocking the church, or like my big brother, you will say that I just don't like preachers.

Again, this is not the case. I love the preacher and the work that the good ones do. I have to share this message, and live with the hardening of your heart towards me.

The plagues will come to your house, and to your church. Your members will start leaving searching for a new church home.

Your members will stop driving across town with no gas in their cars to bring in the tithes.

You will begin to hear the complaints of the people, and nothing you say will satisfy them.

Your children will become ill for no reason, and your wives will become unfaithful as many of you have been for a long time.

Many of you will lose your church as we see in the news every day. Your fame and greatness built over the years will disappear with one news flash.

As the children of Israel left Egypt they took all the money with them so too when your members leave, and your church fails, your fame and fortune will leave also.

God is not pleased! I just came by to warn you.
Of course your members will have to pay for the wrong you led them into, and receive their forty lashes.

But preacher because you have lead them astray you will receive many lashes.

The Lord's Prayer

Problem: The Disciples needed to know how to pray for they saw Jesus doing it all the time. They wanted to know!

Matthew 6:7: *"But when ye pray, use not vain repetitions, as the heathen do: for they think they will be heard for their much speaking."*

Solution: Jesus taught them the Lord's Prayer, and it has everything in it you need to say.

Matthew 6:5 & 9: *"And when thou prayest, thou shalt not be as the hypocrites are: for they love to pray standing in the synagogues and in the corners of the streets, that they may be seen of men. Verily I say unto you, they have their reward."*

Prayer is the process of communicating with God. Like the disciples, your members need to know how to pray.

When they hear many of you pray those long prayers that are mostly done for show, your members try to copy that method of prayer.

This is not what Jesus taught the disciples.

This is not what you should be teaching your members. You don't want to teach them to pray like hypocrites.

They need to know they are talking with the God that loves them, the God that gave His son up to suffer, and die for them.

There is no need to pretend, for God already knows everything, and He already knows if He is going to give you what you request.

Just talk to Him like you talk to a friend who loves you.

Have we come to a point in the 21st century that the Lord's Prayer is no longer effective?

Do we have to pray in public so man can hear how well we pronounce words?

I say preacher you need to do what Jesus told the disciples to do. Teach your members to use the words Jesus taught us to use.

They are enough! No matter what you ask for if God is not ready to provide it to you, He will not.

Playing in the Pulpit

Problem: God is not pleased with what is going on in the Pulpits across America.

I have been charged with telling the Preachers across America and them to the preachers of the world you must change what you are doing, and what you are allowing to be done in the pulpit (holy ground).

God is not pleased with the way the children in your church are being fed and cared for.

God is not pleased with the way you are spending the church funds.

God is not pleased with how you are spending your funds in feeding the sheep you are charged with caring for.

There are members who need financial assistance, and you are not providing it.
You may think you are, but you are not!

Solution: God has a special punishment for the Preacher who leads his children astray.

If you can change you may get less strips across your back, but the punishment is there, and it belongs to the preacher. I am so glad that I am not a preacher!

Preacher, please take care in deciding who you allow to occupy the Holy Ground in your church. This is very important.

Your members determine how they show respect for you based on who you allow to sit up there with you.

The sacredness of this place must be re-established for over the years you have allowed it to become defiled with wrong doing people.

God is not pleased preachers, and He has a special punishment for you if you lead His children astray.

Punishment is payment for a crime or a sin.

It is a crime and a sin for some people to sit up there, to preach from up there. The way people act up there with all the members of your church watching. This is a reflection on you preacher.

Those people who occupy that space wrongfully will pay with 40 stripes, but you preacher will pay with many. Check yourself please!

The preacher who leads God's children astray will be hung over hell fire with a fish hook in their tongue.

You will not burn up; you will just burn. I am so glad I am not a preacher!

Chapter Five

What you must do now?

We have been trained all our lives that God is a God of solution, and God will provide whatever guidance we need to do His will.

Let's review the issues that this book addresses:

1) God is not pleased with the things going on in the pulpits across America.
2) God is not pleased with the manner in which His sheep are being fed and provided for by the preacher.
3) God is not pleased with the way the preacher is using his money in support of God's work.
4) There are some things you can do now to change what is coming.

I know all the seminars you preachers attend each year, where you are taught how to determine who should be in your pulpit. I am referring to the guest you allow to sit there. The guest you allow to speak there.

If you don't have a process that you use in making those decisions, you need one!

The members know when you let a crook come into the pulpit. Your members are not stupid, they live in the community, and they hear things.

Develop the process and let the process decide who sits, and speaks in your church.

As the leader of your church you are responsible for what your members hear.
You are responsible for the people they see up in the pulpit.

I know in my home town the preachers support one another no matter what wrong they have done, and God is not pleased.

There was one preacher who shot his wife when she caught him doing wrong, and the next week he was speaking in one of his friend's church. Wrong being supported by wrong!

There was a preacher convicted of a crime and went to jail. He was not out of jail one year and he was made leader of a ministerial group.

He was representing this group in a meeting seeking funds, and support from the police department.

What were the preachers of that group thinking?

Do you think the police had forgotten they had just let this guy out of jail?

These preachers were supporting one of their own, and making fools of themselves.

Some of the preachers allow known homosexuals to sit, and speak, in the pulpit. Preachers, God is not pleased!

No one in your community is unaware of what you are doing, or allowing it to be done.

What about when you know that you are an abuser of the truth and you know that you are taking money from the church for yourself?

You are the one who is making a mockery of the church, the truth, and the holy ground you occupy.

Don't you fear God, and His punishment?

I think that many of you don't even believe there is a God, or you would not do some of the things you do.

I was told to tell you that God is not pleased. And He has a special punishment awaiting you and all your friends.

Many sheep are following you because they don't know any better, and all that is on you preacher.

I know that I am wasting my time telling you crooks to get out of the business, and out of the pulpit. But I am going to say it anyway!

Many of you preachers are using God's name, and the promises of the Bible to get money for yourselves.

You are telling your members to send you money and promising them that they will be blessed by God for doing so. God is not pleased.

Preachers you have to stop, and think!

You will never get out of the business, or out of the pulpit because you are making a good living. For some of you, a great living.

Some of you have made your wives preachers too, and God is not pleased about that either.

Daddy Melvin said there has to be enough skulls to cover 1500 square miles, so some of you are taking your wives with you. Oh well!

The money that some of you preachers make while at the same time some of the members in your church not having food in their homes or gas in their cars…but they come to church anyway. God is going to bless them in a mighty way!

How do you spend the money that you earn, or steal, or get paid? However you get your money preacher how are you spending it to assist in feeding the children of your flock?

Trust me preacher when I tell you that your members need feeding in a financial way. Remember what we said about "Greed."

The solution is very simple if some of you would just do it. Don't tell me you are doing it because your sheep need feeding.

You are to feed them with some of the money you are building that addition to the church.

Instead of taking so many trips, and vacations, spend some time really getting to know the financial condition of your members.
It would take some of the pressure off you when punishment time comes.

I tell you God is not pleased, and there is special punishment awaiting you preacher!

Get to Know Your Members

Preacher you do not know your members. Some of you may say, "I have 5 thousand members, how can I get to know them all?"

The sheep know their shepherd's voice. They know their shepherd's touch. They know his smell.

We have spoken about how the preachers of old would go to the member's home for a meal. You might want to go back to that, and get to know your members.

Preacher, if you got to know your members better, they would tell you what their needs are, and how you can assist.
They would share with you the things they don't have, that the church can provide.

Instead of adding on to the church you may want to start a drive to get to know your members, and their financial needs.

There were times when two or three shepherds, with all three flocks, had to stay in the same cave during a sand storm, in the field, or desert.

All the sheep and the three shepherds would sleep in the same cave. Each shepherd would take a count of his sheep before he retired for the night.

If any sheep were missing from any of the flocks all of the shepherds would assist in finding the missing sheep.

When the morning came, and the storm had passed, each shepherd would call out and his sheep would come to him, because they knew his voice.

The same way your members know your voice!

If they were sitting in a dark church with no lights, and the preacher started preaching; your members would know if it were you, or some other preacher.

That is a very special bond between two of God's creatures.

Preacher your members need you now! You have to do this because they need your help, and you are going to have to spend some of your money, and the church money to help them.

Preacher you have members that pay their tithes and don't have gas in the car, or food in the house. But they come to church and

pray for a blessing, and you have that blessing in the church account.
But that money is for the conference you are attending next week. Oh well!

You can never provide that blessing if you don't know, or believe they are in need.

They hold you in reverence, they are afraid to ask you for financial assistance.
They are afraid you will talk about them from the pulpit on Sunday in your roundabout way.

They are afraid you will tell your wife, and she will tell the other members, and their business would be all over the church, and all over town.

They would rather go without Preacher! And God is not pleased.

You have members in need who will never schedule an appointment to talk to you.

God told me to tell you to schedule an appointment with all your sheep, and ask them what they need.

Of course some are going to tell a lie, but they got it from you!

It is your responsibility to get to know your members and their needs; and feed them, take care of them.

Find out what they need, and provide it.

Preacher if you schedule the appointment they will come. Many of your members may not need financial assistance but it would make them feel so good to know that you are interested enough in them to schedule a time to speak with them. Oh how special!

If they are not in need of financial assistance, they may now give more to assist in this effort.

In these special meetings with your members you are going to explain what you are doing.

You are going to tell your members they have sisters and brothers in this church that need their help.

You are going to explain that the church is going back to the old-new way of helping one another.

You are going to ask them the hard questions about their finances, and let them know the church is willing to help.

Preacher you are going to find those that need help and are willing to ask for it. You are going to find those who are willing to help even more, in support of their fellow members, in need.

What about those who really need some help and were afraid to ask. This is what the shepherd does: lead them to still water, and make them lie down, in green pastures.

This effort to get to know your members and to provide the financial assistance they need, will bond the members of your flock in a way that is unimaginable.

Preacher before you buy that new bus, before you plan that new addition to the building, before you and some of the special members go on that cruise take that money and see if some of your members need financial assistance.

You are going to find your members would rather spend the church finances helping people close to them than going on that cruise anyway. Try it preacher!
Then provide the help your people need! It would please God so much.

When the Word Gets Around!

Of course, when the word gets around that the preacher and the church leadership are attending to the needs of the members of the church new members will appear and some old members too.

Don't let that sway you preacher, this is God's plan.

You are going to have members of the church against you, because they won't have those to talk about anymore.

They won't have members of the church they can be better than anymore.

This new effort of getting to know the needs of your members, and addressing those needs will change the entire focus of your church ministry.

You can always say you are going back to the way God intended the church to serve the people….like the church of Bible days.

You can say you are going to start acting like a shepherd tending his flock, making sure they are not wanting for anything.

Who is it you are trying to please preacher: the members or God?

When the word gets around that you are a preacher who attends to the real needs of the members of your church some of your old members will come back, and they will come back with a new attitude that will assist you in this new movement.

It may be that you will be able to keep young people in the church when we really start taking care of the people, and their needs.

When the word gets around that God is pleased with the church again that church will be your church, preacher.

That will be a great day!

Chapter Six

Preach On Sister!

Women in the Pulpit

In every church I have attended we have been taught to use the Holy Bible as our source of information.

We are to use the Bible as a reference and guide to get at the root of any biblical question.

There is perhaps no more hotly debated issue in the church today than the issue of women serving as preachers.

In the process of reviewing this issue it is very important to not see this issue as men versus women.
There are many women who believe other women should not serve as preachers and that the Bible places restrictions on the woman. There are men who believe women can serve as preachers. There are men who place no restrictions on women in the church.

This is not an issue of chauvinism, or discrimination.

It is an issue of biblical interpretation.

Based on the research I have done the support for women serving as preachers is just not there.

The research indicates that the issue of women in the pulpit has been debated since the early 1700's in England.

Most of the churches that will be impacted by this book claim their doctrine is based on the bible. People have always been able to find verses that defend their position.

My mentor, Daddy Melvin, taught us to get the question right before we seek an answer.

The question is can a woman preach and/ or pastor a church? Is there a difference between a woman preaching the gospel and pastoring a church?

First let me state my position: It is not an issue that concerns me as much as it may seem. I just wanted to search the scriptures to see what they said.

I am not professionally or spiritually qualified to tell a woman that she can't preach the gospel of our Lord.

I can only relay to the reader of this book what the bible says.

Everywhere I looked I found verses and personal opinions as to having it one way, or the other.

All the information I found pertained to women in leadership roles, and what they accomplished in those positions.

I found information stating that Jesus supported women working in the ministry.

Some claim that the message that Jesus had risen was first carried by women, and this gives the right to preach.

All of the information in support of women preaching used the same bible characters to support their view: most of which confused the issue more than it provided clarification.

Much of it had nothing to do with the proposed question.

The question is not about women in leadership roles nor is it a question pertaining to women working, or teaching, in the church. The question is about women preaching from the pulpit and/or overseeing a church body!

Most church bodies present a position on the subject in their belief structure, and list biblical passages supporting that decision.

The Southern Baptist Convention, which dictates the behavior and belief systems of many Baptist churches, allow women to work in the ministry, as long as they do not hold a position higher than a man.

The Pentecostal church, however, recognizes only men as qualified for church roles.

The Methodist church is widely divided on the subject, and it varies by church.

Some Preachers were passionate on the subject, and defiantly argued either for or against.

All the groups in support asked the same question: "Why is a man better able to spread the word of God than a woman?

They contend that while the Bible does not place men above women in the social order times have changed drastically, and women have become more assertive, and confident in their daily lives.

The groups that are opposed proclaim the exact opposite. They assert the Bible strictly states that women and children should remain silent during service, and should submit to the will of men in all religious decisions.

If we are to accept the Bible as divine law then we have to accept all of what it says, and not just portions that fit our desires.

From the money perspective seminaries accept women as applicants, train and ordain them for the money, knowing that they will most likely not be accepted.

At a minimum in church affairs, the woman's position in the church is subordinate to the man's.

As was stated in the introduction you can stand on whatever side of this issue you choose.

The Bible does not in my estimation clearly say that women can preach from the pulpit, or serve as pastor of a church. It does clearly say that they cannot.

Here is what the word says, and I am through with the issue!

*The Word of God proclaims, *"A woman should learn in quietness and full submission."*

Many preachers do not permit a woman to teach, or to have authority over a man. (1 Timothy 2:11-12).

In the church, God assigns different roles to men and women. This is a result of the way mankind was created, and the way in which sin entered the world. (1 Timothy 2:13-14).

A third common objection is that Paul is only referring to husbands and wives, not men, and women in general. The Greek words in the passage could refer to husbands and wives; however, the basic meaning of the words refers to men, and women.

Further, the same Greek words are used in verses 8-10. Are only husbands to lift up holy hands in prayer without anger, and disputing (verse 8)? Are only wives to dress modestly, have good deeds, and worship God (verses 9-10)? Verses 8-10 clearly refer to all men and women, not only husbands and wives.

There is nothing in the context that would indicate a switch to husbands, and wives in verses 11-14.

Yet another frequent objection to this interpretation of women in ministry is in relation to women who held positions of leadership in the Bible, specifically Miriam, Deborah, and Huldah in the Old Testament.

This objection fails to note some significant factors. First, Deborah was the only female judge among 13 male judges.

Huldah was the only female prophet among dozens of male prophets mentioned in the Bible.

Miriam's only connection to leadership was being the sister of Moses and Aaron.

The two most prominent women in the times of the Kings were Athaliah and Jezebel—hardly examples of godly female leadership.

Most significantly, though, the authority of women in the Old Testament is not relevant to the issue.

The book of 1 Timothy and the other Pastoral Epistles present a new paradigm for the church —the body of Christ—and that paradigm involves the authority structure for the church, not for the nation of Israel, or any other Old Testament entity.

Similar arguments are made using Priscilla and Phoebe in the New Testament.

In Acts 18, Priscilla and Aquila are presented as faithful ministers for Christ.

Priscilla's name is mentioned first, perhaps indicating that she was more "prominent" in ministry than her husband.

However, Priscilla is nowhere described as participating in a ministry activity that is in contradiction to 1 Timothy 2:11-14.

Priscilla and Aquila brought Apollos into their home and they both discipled him, explaining the word of God to him more accurately. (Acts 18:26).

In Romans 16:1, even if Phoebe is considered a "deaconess" instead of a "servant," that does not indicate that Phoebe was a teacher in the church. "Able to teach" is given as a qualification for elders, but not deacons (1 Timothy 3:1-13; Titus 1:6-9). Elders/bishops/deacons are described as the *"husband of one wife," "a man whose children believe,"* and *"men worthy of respect."*

Clearly the indication is that these qualifications refer to men. In addition, in 1 Timothy 3:1-13 and Titus 1:6-9, masculine pronouns are used exclusively to refer to elders/bishops/deacons.

The structure of 1 Timothy 2:11-14 makes the "reason" perfectly clear. Verse 13 begins with "for" and gives the "cause" of Paul's statement in verses 11-12. Why should women not teach, or have authority over men?

Because *"Adam was created first; then Eve! And Adam was not the one deceived; it was the woman who was deceived."* God created Adam first, and then created Eve to be a "helper" for Adam. This order of creation has universal application in the family, (Ephesians 5:22-33) and the church.

The fact that Eve was deceived is also given as a reason for women not serving as pastors, or having spiritual authority over men. This leads some to believe that women should not teach because they are more easily deceived.

That concept is debatable, but if women are more easily deceived, why should they be allowed to teach children, (who are easily deceived) and other women, (who are supposedly more easily deceived)?

That is not what the text says. Women are not to teach men, or have spiritual authority over men, because Eve was deceived. As a result God has given men the primary teaching authority in the church.

Many women excel in gifts of hospitality, mercy, teaching, and helps. Much of the ministry of the local church depends on women. Women in the church are not restricted from public praying, or prophesying (1 Corinthians 11:5), only from having spiritual teaching authority over men. The Bible nowhere restricts women from exercising the gifts of the Holy Spirit (1 Corinthians 12).

Women just as much as men are called to preach to others, to demonstrate the fruit of the Spirit (Galatians 5:22-23). and to proclaim the gospel to the lost (Matthew 28:18-20; Acts 1:8; 1 Peter 3:15).

God has ordained that only men are to serve in positions of spiritual teaching authority in the church. This is not because men are necessarily better teachers, or because women are inferior or less intelligent (which is not the case).

It is simply the way God designed the church to function. Men are to set the example in spiritual leadership—in their lives, and through their words. Women are to take a less authoritative role. Women are encouraged to teach other women (Titus 2:3-5).

The Bible also does not restrict women from teaching children. The only activity women are restricted from is teaching men, or having spiritual authority over them. This logically would preclude women from serving as pastors/preachers.

This does not make women less important, by any means, but rather gives them a ministry focus more in agreement with God's plan, and His gifting of them.

This section (pages 99-105) was taken off the internet by Freddie L. Caldwell Sept. 21, 2010. Author unknown.

"Just did not want the ladies to think they were left out!"

Made in the USA
Charleston, SC
16 July 2013